A Note to Paren

DK READERS is a compelling program for beginning readers, designed in conjunction with leading literacy experts, including Dr. Linda Gambrell, Director of the School of Education at Clemson University. Dr. Gambrell has served on the Board of Directors of the International Reading Association and as President of the National Reading Conference.

Beautiful illustrations and superb full-color photographs combine with engaging, easy-to-read stories to offer a fresh approach to each subject in the series. Each DK READER is guaranteed to capture a child's interest while developing his or her reading skills, general knowledge, and love of reading.

The four levels of DK READERS are aimed at different reading abilities, enabling you to choose the books that are exactly right for your child:

Level 1 – Beginning to read
Level 2 – Beginning to read alone
Level 3 – Reading alone
Level 4 – Proficient readers

The "normal" age at which a child begins to read can be anywhere from three to eight years old, so these levels are only a general guideline.

No matter which level you select, you can be sure that you are helping your child learn to read, then read to learn!

LONDON, NEW YORK, DELHI,
MUNICH, AND MELBOURNE

Project Editor Caryn Jenner
Art Editor Helen Melville
Series Editor Deborah Lock
US Editor Adrienne Betz
Senior Art Editor Clare Shedden
Production Shivani Pandey
Jacket Designer Sophia Tampakopoulos
Picture Research Marie Osborn
Picture Librarians Rachel Hilford,
Sally Hamilton
Illustrator Simone Boni

Reading Consultant
Linda Gambrell, Ph.D.

First American Edition, 2001
03 04 05 10 9 8 7 6 5 4 3 2
Published in the United States by DK Publishing, Inc.
375 Hudson Street, New York, New York 10014

Published in Great Britain by Dorling Kindersley Limited.

A Cataloging-in-Publication record is available
from the Library of Congress.

ISBN 0-7894-7877-3 (hc) ISBN 0-7894-7878-1 (pbk)

Color reproduction by Colourscan, Singapore
Printed and bound in China by L. Rex Printing Co., Ltd.

The publisher would like to thank the following for their kind
permission to reproduce their images:
Positon key: c=center; b=bottom; l=left; r=right; t=top

AKG London: 32br; Bridgeman Art Library, London/New York:
30; Musee Conde, Chantilly, France: 15tr; British Library: 8-9;
British Musuem: 6tl; Corbis: front jacket br, 1br, 4-5, 16-17;
The Art Archive: 32tl; Indiana University, Department of
Underwater Science: 21tr; NASA: 13tr; N.H.P.A.: 18-19;
National Maritime Museum: 2tr, 18t, 32tr;
Gettyone stone: 2br, 21cr.
All other images © Dorling Kindersley
For further imformation see: www.dkimages.com

Discover more at
www.dk.com

DK READERS

BEGINNING
TO READ ALONE
2

The story of
Columbus

Written by Anita Ganeri

DK Publishing, Inc.

In August 1492, a sailor named
Christopher Columbus set out
on an amazing voyage.
He sailed across the
Atlantic Ocean from Spain.

He hoped to bring back gold and treasure from the far lands of Asia that were called the Indies.

In October, Columbus saw land. But this was not the Indies. Columbus had reached some islands near North and South America. To Columbus and his sailors, the Americas were a whole new world.

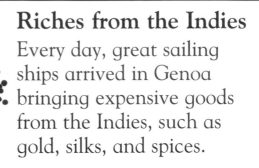

Riches from the Indies
Every day, great sailing ships arrived in Genoa bringing expensive goods from the Indies, such as gold, silks, and spices.

Christopher Columbus was born in 1451 in Genoa, a city in Italy. Genoa was an exciting place to grow up. Columbus liked to watch the ships come and go in the harbor.

He also learned to read, write,
and do simple sums.
He often helped his father,
who worked as a weaver.

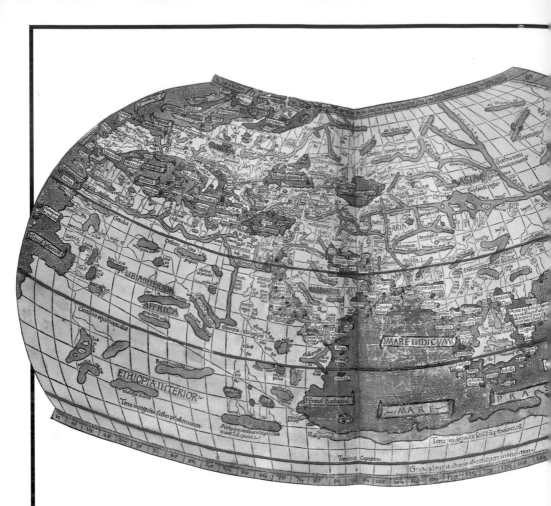

This map of the world was made in 1482. People knew about the continents of Europe, Africa, and Asia. But they did not know the true size and shape of the land.

When Columbus was a teenager, he left home to become a sailor. He wanted to explore the world.

Once, his ship was attacked by pirates. They set the ship on fire. Columbus had to jump into the deep sea. He held onto an oar and swam to shore.

Columbus moved to Portugal. He became a sea captain and sailed to many different places. He and his brother also made maps and charts of the sea.

Columbus married and
had a family.
He still studied his maps and charts.
He gazed out at the Atlantic Ocean.
Columbus had an idea.

In Columbus's time,
merchants and explorers
from Europe always traveled
eastwards to the Indies to buy gold,
silks, and spices.

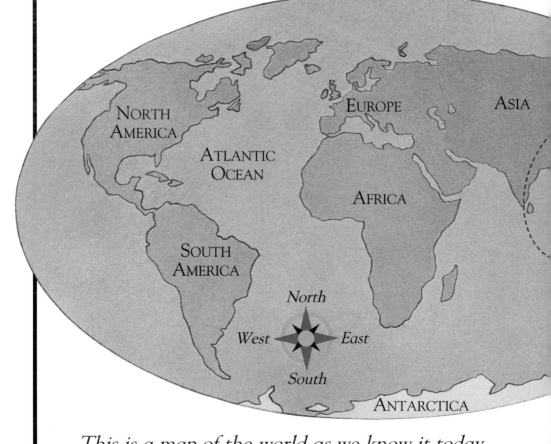

This is a map of the world as we know it today.
It is very different from the old map on page 8.

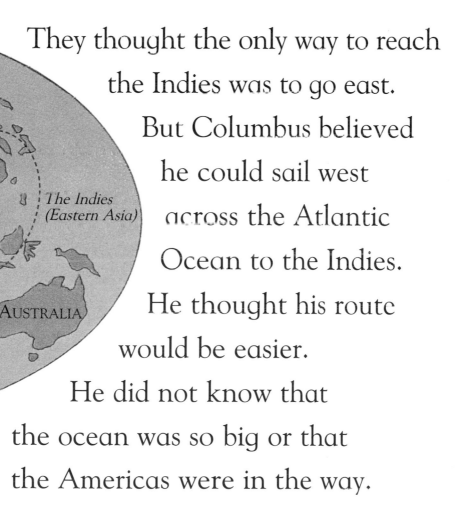

Planet Earth

By Columbus's time, most people knew that Earth was round, not flat. But even Columbus did not know how big our planet really is.

The Indies (Eastern Asia)

AUSTRALIA

They thought the only way to reach the Indies was to go east.

But Columbus believed he could sail west across the Atlantic Ocean to the Indies. He thought his route would be easier.

He did not know that the ocean was so big or that the Americas were in the way.

Columbus needed money to pay
for the ships and crew,
and for food and supplies.
He asked the King of Portugal
for the money.
The King of Portugal said, "No!"
Then Columbus asked the
King and Queen of Spain.
They were interested in his plan,
but told him to wait.

Six years later,
the King and Queen of Spain
finally agreed to help him.
Columbus promised to bring
them riches from his voyage.

Ferdinand and Isabella

King Ferdinand and Queen Isabella of Spain were very powerful. Isabella became a strong supporter of Columbus and his dream.

Columbus bought three ships. They were called the Niña, the Pinta, and the Santa María.

He also bought food and supplies,
such as ropes and nails.
It was hard to find good sailors
for the crew.

Finally, Columbus chose 90 men.
On August 3, 1492, the ships set
sail from Spain into the unknown.

Finding the way
Columbus used a
compass like this
to guide the ships
southwest across
the Atlantic Ocean.

At first, the voyage went well.
The weather was good and
the wind blew the ships along.
The sailors saw strange new sights,
including a whale!

But many weeks passed with
no sight of land.
The crew grew angry and scared.
Perhaps they were lost?
Would they ever get home?
They began to think that
Columbus had made a big mistake.
But he would not turn back.

At last, on October 12, 1492,
the look-out saw a beautiful island.
"Land ahoy!" he shouted.
Columbus claimed the land
for Spain.

Island people

Columbus called the island people "Indians" because he believed he had arrived in the Indies.

He thought they had reached a new part of the Indies.

But this was not true.
The island was in the
Caribbean Sea, near America.
Columbus never admitted
his mistake.
He made the crew sign a paper to
say they had landed in the Indies.
Then they went to look for gold.

Columbus sailed on.

Then disaster struck!

The Santa María sank near an island that Columbus called Hispaniola.

The Taíno people lived on the island.

They were kind and helped the crew.

Columbus chose 39 men
to stay on Hispaniola,
while he and the others sailed home
aboard the Niña and the Pinta.
They reached Spain in March 1493.
Cheering crowds greeted Columbus.
The King and Queen made him
governor of the new lands.

Soon Columbus set sail again.
He took 17 ships and 1200 people.
He wanted to build new cities
and win more riches for Spain.

Columbus sailed to Hispaniola.
But the sailors who had stayed
behind on the island were dead.
They had been cruel to the Taínos,
and the Taínos had fought back.
Columbus and his people sailed
to the other side of Hispaniola,
where they began to build their city.
But many people became sick.
They were very unhappy
and they blamed Columbus.

Columbus explored many islands
in the Caribbean Sea.
Everywhere he went,
he searched for gold.
He made four voyages in total.

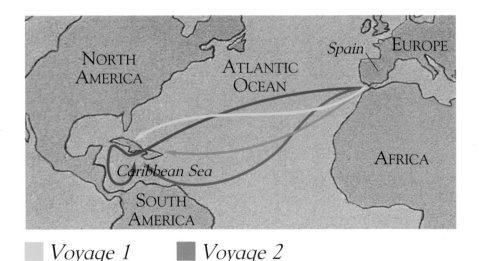

▢ *Voyage 1*		▢ *Voyage 2*	
▢ *Voyage 3*		▢ *Voyage 4*	

During his third trip,
Columbus treated the local
people like slaves and
argued with his own people.

When the King and Queen heard,
they sent someone else
to take over as governor.
Columbus was brought back
to Spain in chains.

The King and
Queen forgave
Columbus and
let him sail across
the ocean one
more time.

On Columbus's last voyage,
fierce storms damaged the ships.
Columbus and his crew
were stranded on an island
that is now called Jamaica.
They traded with the local people,
who gave them food to survive.
After a year on Jamaica,
a rescue ship finally arrived
to take them home.

Back in Spain,
Columbus became sick.
He died on May 20, 1506.

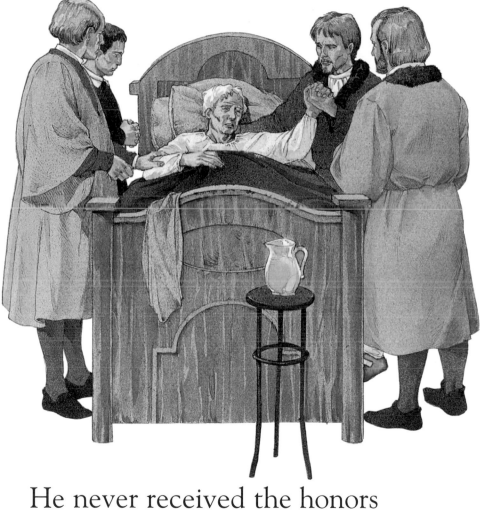

He never received the honors
that he felt he deserved.

Today, Columbus is remembered as a famous explorer. He was daring and brave, but sometimes cruel. He showed that it was possible to sail across the Atlantic Ocean. Columbus did not find a new route to the Indies. Instead, he made contact with a New World.

Many explorers followed Columbus
to the New World.
They found amazing things that
people in Europe had never seen,
such as the food
in this picture.

NORTH
AMERICA

pumpkin

pineapple

corn

Since Columbus,
many people
have come to
the Americas to
make their homes.
His voyages changed
the world forever.

pepper

SOUTH
AMERICA

potatoes

avocado

chocolate

Exploration facts

Vikings from northern Europe may have explored parts of the Americas long before Columbus's famous voyage.

The Taíno people carved long canoes which they used for traveling among the Caribbean islands, and for fishing. Some canoes could carry 100 people.

In Columbus's time, the Atlantic Ocean was called the Ocean Sea. It was believed to be the only ocean. In fact, water covers more than two-thirds of Earth.

There are many islands in the Caribbean Sea. Together they are now known as the West Indies.

Haiti

Dominican Republic

The island of Hispaniola is now divided into two countries called Haiti and the Dominican Republic.

In 1507, a map-maker first used the name America on a map of the New World. It was named after another Italian explorer called Amerigo Vespucci.